# Signature Solos

## 9 All-New Piano Solos by Favorite Alfred Composers

### Selected and edited by Gayle Kowalchyk

Students love getting new music, and teachers love teaching it! What could be more fun than a book of new solos by several favorite Alfred composers? This collection of piano solos was expressly written for the *Signature Solos* series. A variety of different musical styles is found in each of the books.

As editor of this collection, it was a joy for me to play through many solos to find just the right grouping of pieces for each book. I looked for appealing sounds while considering the technical and musical abilities of students at each level. Students are sure to enjoy playing these "signature solos" for friends and family, informally or on recitals.

*Gayle Kowalchyk*

Alfred Music
P.O. Box 10003
Van Nuys, CA 91410-0003
alfred.com

ISBN-10: 1-4706-3216-0
ISBN-13: 978-1-4706-3216-8

Cover Photo
Colored Pencils: © iStock. / Adam Smigielski

# Summer Memories

Catherine Rollin

**Flowing gently and expressively**

# Tango Dance

Martha Mier

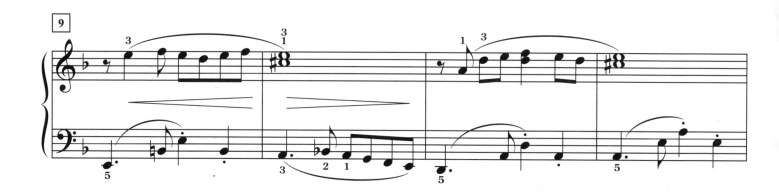

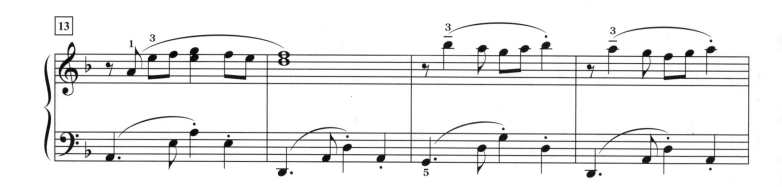

# Port of Charleston

Melody Bober

# Piano Dreams

Robert D. Vandall

# The Wilmington Waltz

Bernadine Johnson

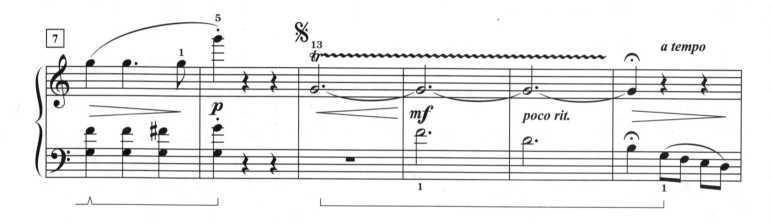

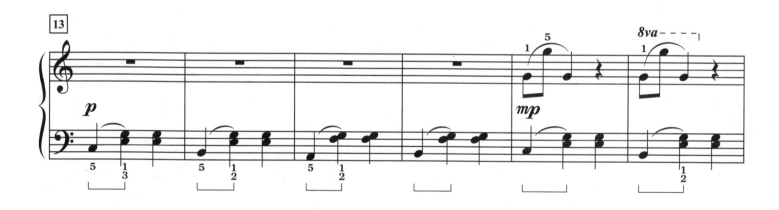

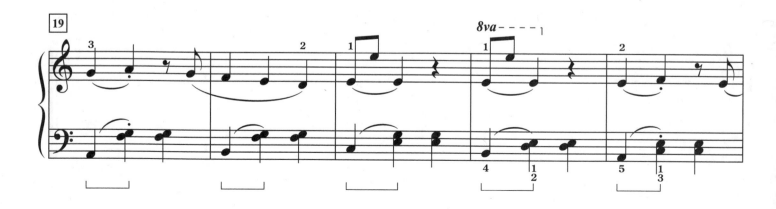

# Love Will See Us Through

Matt Schinske

16

for Madi

# Million Dollar Rag

Judy East Wells

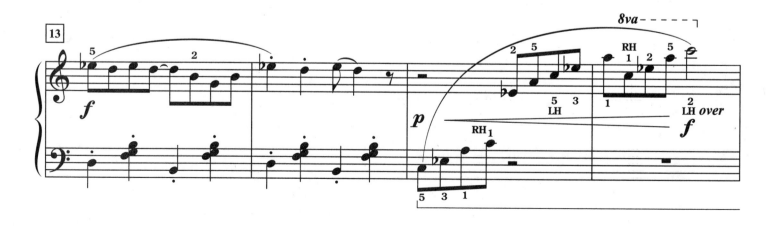

for Erin and Peter

# Deep Blue Water

Wynn-Anne Rossi

# Misty Moon

Rosemary Barrett Byers

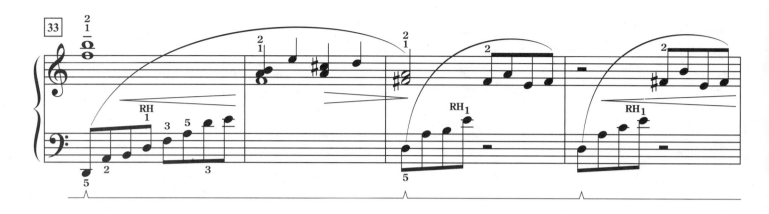

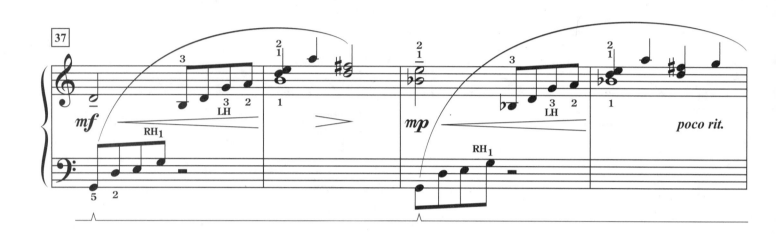

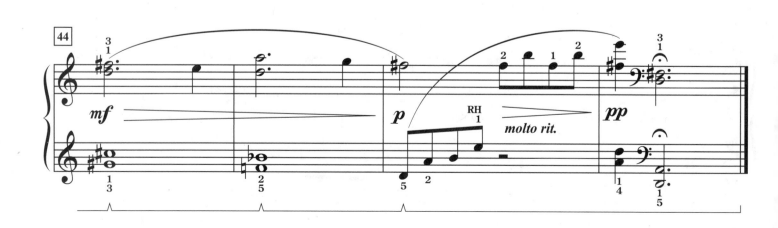